# SUPER LEARNING PROJECTS
## FOR SCHOOLS

**Whole school projects to stimulate
and accelerate the learning of all children
through a 'hands on' approach.**

**Written by Sue Garnett**

**Published by Horizons (UK) Ltd**

# SUPER LEARNING PROJECTS
# CONTENTS

**WHOLE SCHOOL PROJECTS**

**Children's Work Sheets**

**Children's Work Sheets**

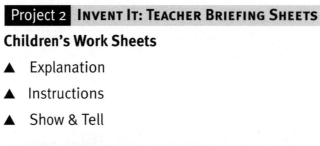

**Children's Work Sheets**

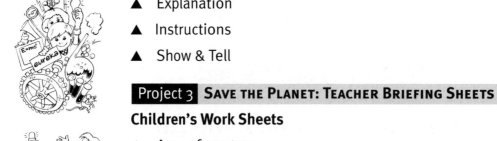

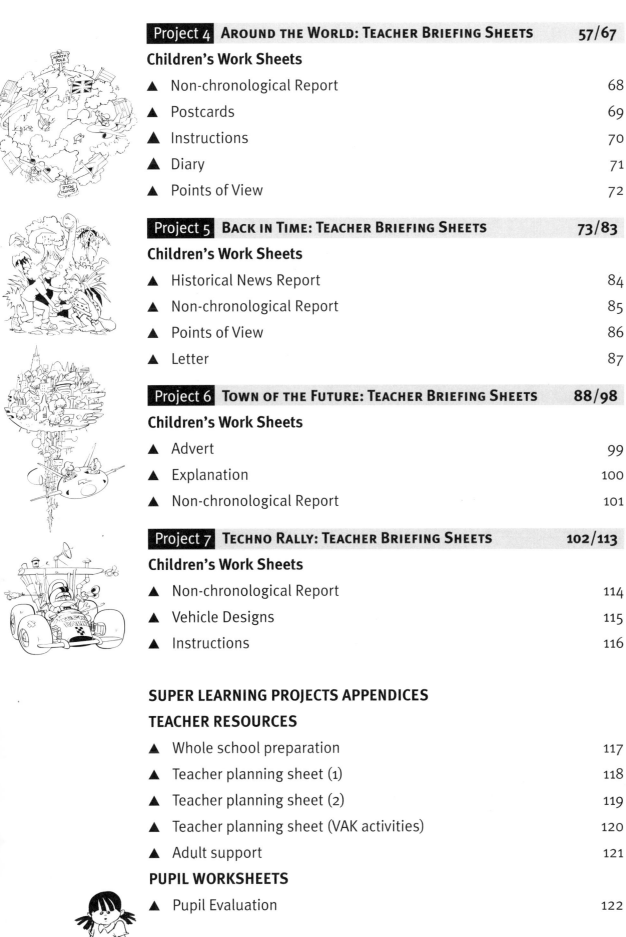

# SUPER LEARNING PROJECTS
## FOR SCHOOLS

First published in 2002
by Horizons (UK) Ltd

Junction 7 Business Park
Blackburn Road
Clayton-le- Moors
Accrington
BB5 5JW

Tel 01254 350035

Written by Sue Garnett
Illustrated and Typeset by John Hutchinson

ISBN 0-9543687-0-3

*'Tell me and I'll forget*
*Show me and I may remember*
*But involve me and I will understand'.*

This book is dedicated to my son Benjamin,
and all the other children in the world who learn best
through practical 'hands on' activities.

Sue Garnett

# SUPER LEARNING PROJECTS
## FOR SCHOOLS
# FOREWORD

**Super Learning Projects is designed to help schools prepare for projects they can undertake with all the pupils in their school.**

### HOW TO USE THE BOOK

The book is divided into two different parts.

### Chapters 1- 5

The first five chapters are for staff. They explain the theory and the background to Super Learning Projects. There is space on each of the pages for staff to take notes.

### Projects 1 - 7

The second part of the book is for teachers to use. There are seven projects. The projects are photocopiable and have space where staff can make notes. There are also photocopiable worksheets for children to use during the project.

Each project looks at different aspects teachers will wish to consider before taking on the project. These include:

- Aims of the project
- What happens
- Places to visit
- The special week
- Curriculum links
- Enterprise

In some of the projects there is additional information which will be useful for that particular project e.g. sponsored event. The projects do not have to be undertaken rigidly, as schools may wish to adapt or omit certain aspects.

The projects have been tried and tested in the classroom with a great deal of success.

The projects can be undertaken with children aged from 4-11 years old. They can be undertaken in any size of school. They can be used with children of all abilities and from different types of cultures.

# CHAPTER 1
# INTRODUCTION

## What are whole school projects?

**Whole school projects are projects the whole school can become involved in. The projects can involve all children and all staff.**

## Why have whole school projects?

Whole school projects are extremely beneficial to the school.

- They enable the staff to develop team work.

- They provide the staff and children with new skills.

- They enable the staff to teach in a more creative way ie still following the National Curriculum objectives but within a theme.

- They enable the staff to find relevance in what they teach.

- They enable the staff to develop a theme and see it through from beginning to end, unlike areas of the curriculum, which may only be covered for several days and then are not carried on until later in the year or in the year to come.

- Children develop new skills.

- Children learn more creatively and in a 'hands on' way.

- Children develop confidence and self esteem.

- Children can develop team work.

- Children can see the relevance in their learning.

- Children can see something through from beginning to end.

## How do whole school projects fit in with the curriculum?

- The staff is still able to follow the National Curriculum.

- They follow the National Curriculum with a thematic approach.

- They can plan the project on a variety of planning sheets which still have the same headings as they would use normally i.e. objectives, resources, activities, assessment, evaluation (See planning sheets at the back of the book).

## Practical learning

- Whole school projects encourage practical learning.

- They enable the teacher to steer away from photocopiable sheets and text books.

- They encourage practical, 'hands on' learning where the children are doing rather than merely writing or listening.

- They encourage the children in the class who have special needs and give them confidence.

- They teach the children new skills which can be applied in later life.

- They improve behaviour because children are actively involved.

- Research says that children are more likely to learn and remember if they are actively involved.

May be photocopied for classroom use only Published by Horizons (UK) Ltd

# CHAPTER 2

# PREPARING FOR A WHOLE SCHOOL PROJECT

## School Climate

- School climate is paramount to the success of a whole school project.

- All the staff need to be on board. It is better to wait than rush in before staff and children are ready, willing and able.

If a school has never undertaken whole school projects, it is important to build up to them.

## This can be done by:

- Having a day away from the curriculum e.g. a project day following a school visit or after visitors and performers have been in school. On this day teachers do not plan or teach in the same way. They are encouraged to use other planning methods and do more 'hands on' learning.

- Visiting schools where successful projects have been undertaken.

- Inviting teachers to staff meetings from schools where projects have been undertaken successfully.

- Attending conferences where the speakers focus on whole school projects.

## Timing

- Timing is vital.

- Whole school projects can be done at any time of year, although steering away from special events is a factor to consider i.e. annual tests, festive occasions.

## Meetings

- Staff meetings will need to be arranged in order for everyone to be clear about the project.

- The Project Co-ordinator needs to have read the booklet and be fully aware of the implications for the school.

- Meetings will need to be arranged well in advance in order for staff to plan the event, organise visits, buy resources and approach partners.

## Planning

- Staff will need to be clear about the planning sheets they will use.

- The planning sheets should be seen as a tool not extra unnecessary work. (See sheets at the back of the book).

# CHAPTER 3
# PARTNERS & SPONSORS

## Partners and Sponsors

- The school approaches local business partnerships to ask for funding (the school may have to fill in a bid for support).

- Partners and sponsors are approached to support the project:
  - local companies eg retailers, factories
  - trust funds
  - parents
  - governors
  - public services e.g. police, health

- The partners support the school by giving:
  - Time i.e. working in the classroom with the children.
  - Expertise i.e. coming into school and explaining how their product is made.
  - Resources i.e. donating resources for the children to use e.g. ingredients to make the sweets, clay to make the models.

- The school can ask a company who is going to give support to be their School Business Partners. Once the school has a School Business Partner, this partnership can be developed, resulting in further funding for the school and funding for future projects. The school can approach other schools who have School Business Partners for advice.

- Partners need to be approached well in advance. They can be sent an initial letter that can then be followed up by a phone call.

- Letters need to be written to the sponsors to inform them of the role they can play (See example letters at the back of the book) e.g. letters to companies asking for a tour of their premises, letters to companies asking for resources, letters to public services, parents and governors asking for support in the classroom.

- The sponsors are informed of the benefits they will gain from the partnership e.g. local newpapers, local radio, logo on advertising etc.

- The partners are invited to visit the school prior to the event.

- The partners are invited to the special event at the end of the week.

- The local newspaper and local radio can be invited to report on the special week.

# CHAPTER 4

# ENTERPRISE

Many of the projects in the book are linked with Enterprise. The projects introduce children into how companies work and prepare them for the future and the outside world of work.

## The children learn:

- How to set up a company
- How companies raise money with company shares
- Fund raising
- Research skills
- Supply and demand
- Budgeting
- Marketing skills
- Design and making skills
- How to persuade people to buy their products
- How to advertise their goods
- How to make a profit and use that profit for new business developments

# CHAPTER 5

# GETTING STARTED

- Read through the project you are interested in.
- Have a staff meeting to talk about the project.
- Link the project with your School Development Plan or Whole School Project.
- Talk about the benefits to the school, staff and children.
- Go through the ideas for the project. Ask the staff for additional ideas.
- Set a date for the project (give lots of time for planning and organisation).
- Approach partners and sponsors for advice and funding.
- Visit a school that has undertaken the project or invite them to your school to talk about it.
- Use the planning sheets for support.

### PROJECT 1

# WORLD OF WORK

### WORLD OF WORK

# Aims of the Project

● For the school to develop partners in the local community.

● For the staff to develop team work.

● For the staff to find creative ways of teaching.

● For the staff to find relevance in what they teach.

● For the staff to develop new skills.

● For the children to develop new skills.

● For the children to experience 'hands on' learning.

● For the children to develop confidence and self esteem.

● For the children to develop a positive outlook for the future.

## WORLD OF WORK

# What happens?

- Classes convert into a company for a week.

........................................................................................................

- They visit a company prior to the week to get ideas.

........................................................................................................

- The children buy shares in their company by raising money through a sponsored event.

........................................................................................................

- They buy resources for their company.

........................................................................................................

- They design and make products.

........................................................................................................

- They invite partners into school to help them.

........................................................................................................

- They advertise the products.

........................................................................................................

- They sell the products.

........................................................................................................

........................................................................................................

**WORLD OF WORK**

# Sponsored Event

- ● Sponsored Event.

- ● To raise money to buy the materials for the companies the children have a sponsored event.

- ● The children take home sponsor forms to their parents explaining the project.

- ● The staff organise the sponsored event
  e.g. obstacle course, skipping marathon, sponsored run, word search, sponsored spell.

- ● Any child who raises money for his or her company receives a share certificate.

- ● If the school has a School Business Partner, they can ask the company to match fund the money they have raised.

- ● The staff purchase materials for their companies.

## WORLD OF WORK

# Places to Visit

**Each class visits a company to get ideas for the product they are going to make.
Examples:**

● **Retailers**
e.g. stationers, card shops.

● **Food retailers**
e.g. supermarkets, bakers, sweet makers.

● **Manufacturers**
e.g. rosette making company, book mark company, badge makers, tee shirt printers.

● **Craft shops**
e.g. making salt dough, pottery.

● **Museums**

**WORLD OF WORK**

# Setting up the Companies

● **Each class decides on the product they want to make**
  e.g. sweets, badges, book marks, rosettes, pottery, fridge magnets, printed tee shirts.

● **They work out the cost of materials and how much they will have to charge to make a profit.**

● **They decide on a name for their company.**

● **They visit a company to see how the product is made or ask the company to visit school.**

● **Each class is set up to look like a company**
  e.g. Reception area with receptionist and signing in book, production areas,
  packaging, rest areas, etc.

## WORLD OF WORK

# The Special Week

**FIRST DAY**

● Special assembly to introduce the week.

● Classes visit companies / Companies visit schools.

**ON GOING**

● Classes design, make and advertise their product.

● Lessons are cross curricular.

● Partners come into school and support the companies.

**PENULTIMATE DAY**

● Advertising campaign, partners and parents invited.

**FINAL DAY**

● Market, products go on sale, companies count their profits.

### WORLD OF WORK

# Advertising Campaign

Each class produces an advertising campaign to advertise their product.

## POSTERS

● Companies design posters which they display around school.

## SANDWICH BOARDS

● Companies make sandwich boards and advertise their product at play times.

## BUSINESS CARDS

● Companies make cards to give out to people.

● **Companies produce an advert to show to parents, partners and children. It has to be short.**
i.e. ten minutes. They can use song, dance, persuasion, role play.

**WORLD OF WORK**

# Enterprise/Market Day

- **The products need to be finished by the morning of the last day.**

- **On the last afternoon, class representatives set up tables in the hall to display their products.**

- **The goods are priced to make a profit.**

- **The class set up their advertising** e.g. posters, sandwich boards.

- **Parents, partners and children are invited to buy from the companies.**

- **The companies count their profits.**

- **The profits can be used to further develop their company and buy more materials or be spent on the share holders in the company**
  e.g. a treat for the children or something that they would like for the classroom.

## WORLD OF WORK
# Literacy
### KEY STAGE 1

### ■ READING

- ● Read non-fiction books and learn about the difference between fiction and non-fiction books.

- ● Read recipe books.

- ● Read instruction books e.g. How to make a...

- ● Read non-fiction books about jobs and places of work.

- ● Use dictionaries to find words associated with the topic.

### ■ WRITING

- ● Make class dictionaries on the topic.

- ● Write lists of things you need for making the products.

- ● Write lists of words associated with your product.

- ● Write instructions for making your product.

- ● Draw and make labels and captions for the products.

- ● Write a recount of the visit to the company.

- ● Write a glossary for the product you are making.

- ● Produce simple flow charts.

- ● Write simple non-chronological reports about the topic that is being studied.

### ■ SPEAKING AND LISTENING

- ● Show and tell - the product you have made.

- ● Explain how you made the product.

- ● Ask questions about each other's products.

# KEY STAGE 2

### READING

● Understand the difference between fiction and non-fiction books.

● Read a variety of non-fiction books e.g. recipe books, instruction books.

● Locate information using contents and indexes.

● Identify and highlight or note key words from a text.

● Research the topic being undertaken.

### WRITING

● Make notes from information books in different forms e.g. flow charts, key words and lists.

● Write non-chronological reports e.g. different types of book marks.

● Use technical language when writing reports.

● Write instructions for making your product e.g. make a book mark.

● Write a recount of a visit to a company.

● Make alphabetically ordered texts for your product.

● Write an explanation of how you made your product.

● Write a point of view about why your product is the best.

● Design adverts selling your product – use exaggerated language.

● Write a letter to a company asking them to sell your product.

● List cues for a talk you will be giving to the visitors at the end of the week about your product.

● Write a commentary for TV or radio on your product.

● Write a balanced argument on the good/bad points of the product.

### SPEAKING AND LISTENING

● Discuss the product to be made e.g. materials, quantity, cost.

● Listen to other people's opinions about what product should be made.

● Give clear instructions for making the product.

## WORLD OF WORK

# Art Ideas

## KNOWLEDGE, SKILLS AND UNDERSTANDING

Explore, develop ideas, investigate and make, evaluate and develop, knowledge and understanding

## BREADTH OF STUDY

## KEY STAGE 1/2 IDEAS

- Colour mixing – choosing colours for the products.

- Draw designs for products, freehand, on the computer, label.

- Explore ideas eg What type of badge should I make? What shape? What colour? What size?

- Investigate materials for making the product
  e.g. card or paper? Felt or fabric? Clay or plasticene?

- Use different tools to make the product.

- Design and draw posters, adverts, business cards, sandwich boards.

- Design leaflets to advertise the product.

- Design a certificate for shares in the company.

- Design packaging for the product. Think about size and material.
  Measure and cut to the correct size.

## WORLD OF WORK

# Design Technology

### KNOWLEDGE, SKILLS AND UNDERSTANDING

Develop, plan and communicate ideas, work with tools and equipment,
evaluate processes and products, knowledge and understanding of materials.

### BREADTH OF STUDY

### KEY STAGE 1/2 IDEAS

- Badges

- Bean bags

- Board games

- Bookmarks

- Candles

- Comb cases

- Fridge magnets

- Jewellery

- Jigsaws

- Night light pottery

- Pop up cards

- Puppets

- Rosettes

- Soap

- Tee shirts

- **Work with a variety of tools** e.g. brushes, scissors, glue.

- **Work with a variety of materials**
  e.g. fabrics, wood, card, clay, plasticene, salt dough, cooking ingredients, magnets.

## WORLD OF WORK

# Numeracy

## KNOWLEDGE, SKILLS AND UNDERSTANDING

Explore, develop ideas, investigate and make, evaluate and develop, knowledge and understanding

## BREADTH OF STUDY

## KEY STAGE 1 IDEAS

- **Use a ruler to draw and measure lines to the nearest cm for your design.**

- **Compare two lengths** e.g. How long is your design, how long is the other?

- **Use language to describe 2D and 3D shapes i.e. the shapes of the designs you have designed** e.g. it is a sphere.

- **Estimate, measure and compare the designs you have drawn** e.g. compare the size of one design to another.

- **Tally chart of items made and sold etc.**

- **Count the products, put into groups according to colour and size.**

## KEY STAGE 2 IDEAS

- **Problem solving** e.g. How many do we need to sell to make a profit?

- **Profit and loss based on different costs.**

- **Handling data** e.g. How many are we going to sell?

- **Use fractions and decimals to get accurate measurements of the designs you are drawing.**

- **Use standard units of measure to draw your designs.**

- **Identify lines of symmetry in your designs.**

- **Identify right angles and parallel lines in the designs you draw.**

- **Visualize how your design will look in 3D from a 2D drawing.**

- **Use a protractor to draw and measure angles of your designs.**

- **Draw graphs** e.g. to show profits at different prices.

# WORLD OF WORK
## Information about the Company

**My Name**

**Name of our company**

**What we are going to sell**

**What we will need**

●

●

●

●

**How long it will take us to make a product**

**How many we can make**

**How much they will be sold at**

**How much money we can make**

**How we will spend the profits?**

    Published by Horizons (UK) Ltd

# WORLD OF WORK
## Becoming a Company

Name _____ Class _____

**Name of our Company** _____

**How we will convert the classroom into a company**

### THE WALLS

### REST AREA

### RECEPTION AREA

### PRODUCTION AREA

# WORLD OF WORK
## How to Make the Product

**Name** ............................................    **Class** ............................................

### WHAT I AM GOING TO MAKE
**What I need**

- ............................................
- ............................................
- ............................................
- ............................................
- ............................................
- ............................................

### MY PRODUCT

### HOW TO MAKE IT

1. ............................................
............................................
............................................

2. ............................................
............................................
............................................
............................................

3. ............................................
............................................
............................................
............................................

4. ............................................
............................................
............................................

5. ............................................
............................................
............................................
............................................

6. ............................................
............................................
............................................
............................................

# WORLD OF WORK
## Product Designs

**Name** ............................................     **Class** ............................................

**Product** ...........................................................................................................

# WORLD OF WORK
## Advertising Ideas

**Name** .................................................. **Class** ..................................................

## BUSINESS CARD

## POSTER

## SANDWICH BOARD

## TELEVISION ADVERTISING

### PROJECT 2

# INVENT IT

### 2:2 AIMS OF THE PROJECT
### 2:3 WHAT HAPPENS
### 2:4 THE SPECIAL WEEK
### 2:5 DISPLAY DAY
### 2:6 CURRICULUM IDEAS

**INVENT IT**

# Aims of the Project

● **For the children to invent a new product.**

● **For the children to experience 'hands on' learning.**

● **For the children to develop confidence and self esteem.**

● **For the staff and children to develop new skills.**

● **For the school to develop partners in the local community.**

● **For the staff to develop team work.**

● **For the staff to find creative ways of teaching.**

● **For the staff to find relevance in what they teach.**

**INVENT IT**

# What happens?

- **Each class chooses a theme for what type of invention they would like to make**
  e.g. toys for a baby, electric games, support for deaf or blind, holders for…,
  containers to keep food hot, improved shopping bags.

- **They read books, visit the library and go on the internet to find out more about what they want to make.**

- **They visit a company prior to the week to get ideas.**

- **They design and make their inventions.**

- **They invite partners into school to help them.**

- **They set up displays in the hall selling their inventions.**

- **They invite the rest of the school and partners to visit the displays.**

- **Each class gives a talk to the rest of the school on their invention and why people should buy it.**

- **They can invite partners, companies to bid for the models which they would then take back to their firm to display.**

### INVENT IT

# The Special Week

**FIRST DAY**
● Special assembly to introduce the project.

.................................................................................

● Classes visit companies.

.................................................................................

**ON GOING**
● Classes design and make their inventions.

.................................................................................

● Lessons are cross curricular.

.................................................................................

● Partners come into school and support the companies.

.................................................................................

**FINAL DAY**
● The inventions are displayed in the hall.

.................................................................................

● Parents and partners are invited to see the displays.

.................................................................................

● The inventions are sold or auctioned to the highest bidder.

.................................................................................

## INVENT IT
# Display Day

● The products need to be finished by the penultimate day.

● On the morning of the last day, class representatives set up tables in the hall to display their inventions.

● The inventions will be labelled and have an explanation as to what they do.

● Parents and partners are invited to look at the displays.

● Each class talks about their invention and tries to sell it to the listeners.

● After the class talks, visitors are encouraged to buy the inventions or there could be an auction and inventions could be sold to the highest bidders.

● After the event a display area can be set up in the entrance hall or in classrooms.

PROJECT 2:5

## INVENT IT

# Literacy

## KEY STAGE 1

### READING

● Read non-fiction books and learn about the difference between non-fiction and fiction.

● Read non-fiction books about famous inventors and inventions.

● Look at catalogues and read about new products.

● Use dictionaries to find words associated with the topic.

### WRITING

● Make class dictionaries on the topic.

● Write lists of things you need for making the inventions.

● Write lists of words associated with inventions.

● Write instructions for making a model.

● Draw and make labels and captions for the models.

● Write a recount of the visit to the company.

● Write a glossary for the invention you are making.

● Produce simple flow charts.

● Write simple non-chronological reports about the topic that is being studied e.g. children's toys.

### SPEAKING AND LISTENING

● Ask questions about the invention.

● Show and Tell i.e. show your invention and explain how it works.

● Give views and opinions on other people's inventions.

## KEY STAGE 2

### READING

● Understand the difference between fiction and non-fiction books.

● Locate information using contents and indexes.

● Identify and highlight or note key words from a text.

● Research the topic being undertaken.

### WRITING

● **Make notes from information books in different forms** e.g. flow charts, key words and lists.

● **Write non chronological reports** e.g. children's toys.

● **Write instructions for making inventions** e.g. how you made your toy.

● **Write a recount of a visit to a company.**

● **Make alphabetically ordered texts for your invention.**

● **Write newspaper reports about your invention**
  e.g. giving information on how it will change people's lives and what people think of it.

● **Write explanations of how your invention works.**

● **Use technical language when writing reports and explanations.**

● **Write a point of view about why your invention is the best,**
  **use language to move the argument on.**

● **Design adverts selling your invention.**

● **Write a letter to a company asking them to buy your invention.**

● **List cues for a talk you will be giving to the visitors at the end of the week about your invention.**

● **Write a commentary for TV or radio on your invention.**

● **Write a balanced argument on the good/bad points of the invention.**

### SPEAKING AND LISTENING

● **Hot Seat - others to ask questions about the invention.**

● **Plan your talk to give to the visitors about your invention.**

## INVENT IT

# Science

## KNOWLEDGE, SKILLS AND UNDERSTANDING

### Scientific enquiry, life processes and living things, materials, physical processes

## BREADTH OF STUDY

## KEY STAGE 1/2 IDEAS

● **Electricity** – make games and toys using simple circuits with batteries, wires, bulbs and switches.

● **Forces** – make games and toys which require pushing or pulling.

● **Light & Sound** – make musical toys which make different sounds, change the pitch and loudness.

● **Materials** – Make inventions after investigating the types of material to be used, how the shapes of objects can be changed by bending and stretching.

● **Draw designs and diagrams.**

● **Investigate what may happen when you make the invention.**

● **Test ideas using evidence from observations and measurement.**

● **Ask questions** e.g. What will happen if I take away...?

**INVENT IT**

# Design Technology

## KNOWLEDGE, SKILLS AND UNDERSTANDING

Develop, plan and communicate ideas, work with tools
and equipment, evaluate processes and products, knowledge and understanding of materials

## BREADTH OF STUDY

## KEY STAGE 1/2 IDEAS

● **Design and make electric buzzer games.**

● **Design and make aids for the deaf or blind.**

● **Design and make 3D games.**

● **Design and make magnetic games.**

● **Design and make fun things.**

● **Design and make toys for babies and toddlers.**

● **Design and make toys for an animal.**

● **Design and make strong/fold away bags.**

● **Design and make 3D jigsaws, cube games.**

● **Work with a variety of tools** e.g. brushes, scissors, glue.

● **Work with a variety of materials**
  e.g. fabrics, wood, card, clay, electrical equipment, magnets, plastic.

**INVENT IT**

# Numeracy

## KNOWLEDGE, SKILLS AND UNDERSTANDING

Number, shape space and measure, handling data

### BREADTH OF STUDY

### KEY STAGE 1 IDEAS

● **Use a ruler to draw and measure lines to the nearest cm.**

● **Compare two lengths e.g. how long?**

● **Use language to describe 2D and 3D shapes i.e. the shapes of the invention you have designed** e.g. it is a triangular pyramid.

● **Estimate, measure and compare shapes you have drawn** e.g. compare the size of another model someone else is making.

### KEY STAGE 2 IDEAS

● **Use fractions and decimals to get accurate measurements of the invention you are drawing.**

● **Use standard units of measure to draw your invention.**

● **Identify lines of symmetry in your invention.**

● **Identify right angles and parallel lines in your invention.**

● **Visualize how the invention will look in 3D from a 2D drawing.**

● **Use a protractor to draw and measure angles of your designs.**

● **Identify shapes on designs.**

● **Name the 3D shapes.**

## Invent It
# Explanation

**Name** ............................................................    **Class** ....................................................................

**My Invention** ...........................................................

**Who it is for** ...........................................................

**What it will do** ...........................................................

**How it will work** ...........................................................

..................................................................................

..................................................................................

..................................................................................

..................................................................................

..................................................................................

..................................................................................

..................................................................................

..................................................................................

..................................................................................

**How it will work**

## Invent It
# Instructions
## How to make It

**Name** ......................................................  **Class** ..........................................................

**My invention** .............................................

**How to make it** ..........................................

## What I will need

● ..........................................................

● ..........................................................

● ..........................................................

● ..........................................................

● ..........................................................

## My Invention

## How to make it

1. ..........................................................

2. ..........................................................

3. ..........................................................

4. ..........................................................

5. ..........................................................

6. ..........................................................

### INVENT IT
# Show and Tell
## MY INVENTION

**Name** .................................................. **Class** ..................................................

## What it does

```
.................................................................................
.................................................................................
.................................................................................
.................................................................................
.................................................................................
.................................................................................
.................................................................................
.................................................................................
```

## Why is it brilliant? Why should you have one?

```
.................................................................................
.................................................................................
.................................................................................
.................................................................................
.................................................................................
.................................................................................
.................................................................................
```

## PROJECT 3

# SAVE THE PLANET

**SAVE THE PLANET**

# Aims of the Project

- For the children to learn about the world and how they can make it a better place.

- For the children to develop new skills.

- For the children to experience 'hands on' learning.

- For the children to develop confidence and self esteem.

- For the school to develop partners in the local community.

- For the staff to develop team work.

- For the staff to find creative ways of teaching.

- For the staff to find relevance in what they teach.

- For the staff to develop new skills.

**SAVE THE PLANET**

# What happens?

● **Each class focuses on a problem in our world** e.g. pollution, endangered species, rain forests.

● **They read books, visit the library and go on the internet.**

● **They visit places prior to the week to get ideas.**

● **The children spend the week converting their classroom into an exhibition with displays, photos, newspaper cuttings, friezes of:**

  ▲ **Where their problem occurs.**

  ▲ **Facts and figures.**

  ▲ **The damage it does.**

  ▲ **What is being done about it.**

  ▲ **What children can do about it.**

● **They do 'hands on' practical activities and make souvenirs.**

● **They invite partners into school to help them** e.g. school nurse.

● **They invite the rest of the school to visit their exhibition and enterprise on 'Save the Planet' on the Friday.**

● **They make money by selling gifts** e.g. save the whale badges, face paintings of endangered species, pen pot holders from recycled materials.

## SAVE THE PLANET

# Places to Visit/Visitors

## POLLUTION

- Canals

- Rivers

- Sea side resorts

- Power Stations

- City centres – traffic, noise

- Water Authorities – sewage works

## ENDANGERED SPECIES

- Zoos

- Wild life parks

- Monkey sanctuaries

- National Parks

- RSPB centres

## RECYCLING

- Recycling plants

- Paper mills

- Waste paper factories

**SAVE THE PLANET**

# The Special Week

**FIRST DAY**
- Special assembly to introduce the week.

- Classes visit places of interest and companies.

**ON GOING**
- Lessons are cross curricular and 'hands on'.

- Pupils make souvenirs to sell at the open day.

- Partners come into school and support the pupils.

**FINAL DAY**
- Each class visits the exhibitions.

- Staff and children show the other pupils around.

- Visitors are encouraged to buy souvenirs to further the classes' involvement
  e.g. the class may then sponsor an animal at a zoo or join a national society.

- In a special assembly the following week each class tells the others what they plan to do to continue their support for their area of interest
  e.g. join a society, sponsor an animal, collect litter.

- Children are encouraged to make comments in a special book which will then be collated for display purposes and to show forthcoming ideas and plans for saving the planet.

- If the school has a web site they can develop a page on 'Save the Planet' which can be shared with other schools.

SAVE THE PLANET

# Exhibition/Enterprise

- Each class invites the other to visit their exhibition and enterprise.
  The children tour each exhibition looking at what there is and talk to representatives from the class.

  - look at the displays ........................................................................................................
  - look at the posters ........................................................................................................
  - look at the photographs ........................................................................................................
  - look at facts and figures ........................................................................................................
  - look at reports ........................................................................................................
  - look at video evidence ........................................................................................................
  - look at the plans for the future ........................................................................................................

- **The children can buy souvenirs** e.g. postcards, models, badges.

- After visiting each exhibition, classes can contribute to a 'Save the Planet' Book which will then be put on display in the school.

- The classes use the money to pay for joining a society or sponsoring an animal in a zoo etc.

## SAVE THE PLANET

# Literacy

## KEY STAGE 1

### READING

● Read non-fiction books and learn about the difference between non-fiction and fiction.

● Read non-fiction books about global issues.

● Use dictionaries to find words associated with the topic.

● Make class dictionaries on the topic.

### WRITING

● Write lists of words associated with your focus.

● Draw and make labels and captions for your focus area.

● Write a recount of the visit to the company.

● Write a glossary for the focus of your topic.

● Produce simple flow charts.

● Write simple non chronological reports about the topic that is being studied
e.g. rainforest creatures.

### SPEAKING AND LISTENING

● Read aloud information from non-fiction books.

● Ask questions about the topic.

● Listen to people's views about the topic and what should be done about it.

## KEY STAGE 2

### READING

- Understand the difference between fiction and non-fiction books.

- Read books about pollution, endangered species, rainforests, erosion, recycling.

- Locate information using contents and indexes.

- Identify and highlight or note key words from a text.

- Research the topic being undertaken.

### WRITING

- **Make notes from information books in different forms** e.g. flow charts, key words and lists.

- **Write non chronological reports** e.g. different types of pollution.

- Write a recount of a visit to a company.

- Make alphabetically ordered texts for your topic.

- Write newspaper reports about your area of concern
  e.g. giving information about it and what people think of it.

- Design adverts for your area of concern.

- Write a commentary for TV or radio on your problem.

- Write a point of view about why we should do something about the problem you are considering.

- Write a balanced argument for why we should/should not support your cause

- Write explanations of a process
  e.g. why smoking causes health problems, how pollution kills river life.

### SPEAKING AND LISTENING

- Prepare a talk for different audiences.

- Prepare a 'Power Point'© presentation on your issue.

- Give clear views and opinions with evidence.

- **Take on different roles and express an opinion** e.g. hunter, lumberjack, native, park warden.

PROJECT 3:7

## SAVE THE PLANET

# Geography

### KNOWLEDGE, SKILLS AND UNDERSTANDING

Enquiry and skills, knowledge and understanding of places, patterns and processes, environmental change and sustainable development

## BREADTH OF STUDY

## KEY STAGE 1/2

- **Ask geographical questions** e.g. What would it be like to live in a rainforest? What do I think about pollution? What could I do to help?

- **Observe and record** e.g. identify the layers in the rainforest.

- **Express their own views** e.g. What do you think about hunting?

- **Use geographical vocabulary** e.g. equator, north pole.

- **Make maps** e.g. the river, canal, the seaside.

- **Use atlases, globes, maps** e.g.find the rainforests, find animals around the world which are becoming endangered.

- **Collect evidence** e.g. numbers of endangered species.

- **Decision making skills** e.g. What measures need to be taken to save the species?

- **Recognize changes** e.g. rainforest destruction.

- **Recognize how the environment may be improved** e.g. by the canal or seaside, collecting litter, factory pollution.

- **Recognize and understand patterns** e.g. rainforest distribution.

- **Recognize how people can improve or damage the environment** e.g. river and sea pollution.

- **Identify what a place is like** e.g. the rainforest.

- **Identify opportunities for sustaining the environment** e.g. whole school project on 'Save the Planet,' join a society, sponsored event to raise money.

## SAVE THE PLANET

# Art & Design

## KNOWLEDGE, SKILLS AND UNDERSTANDING

Explore, develop ideas, investigate and make, evaluate and develop, knowledge and understanding

## BREADTH OF STUDY

## KEY STAGE 1 IDEAS

- **Vegetable prints.**

- **Badges** e.g. Save the Panda.

- **Posters** e.g. Don't drop litter, Smoking damages your health.

- **Animal masks.**

- **Wax resist pictures** e.g. rainforest, animals.

- **Mirror patterns of engangered species.**

- **Moving animals using paper fasteners.**

- **Life size paintings of endangered species.**

- **Life size rainforest in the corner of the classroom.**

- **3D model of the sea side using papier mache.**

- **Collages** e.g. litter.

- **Maps of the rainforests and endangered animals.**

- **Design a page on the school web site for Save the Planet.**

- **Design a recyling system** e.g. recycle bin.

- **Leaflets to give to parents and the local community.**

SAVE THE WORLD

# Science

## KNOWLEDGE, SKILLS AND UNDERSTANDING

Scientific enquiry, life processes and living things, materials, physical processes

## BREADTH OF STUDY

## KEY STAGE 1/2 IDEAS

- **Life processes/humans and other animals/green plants –Keeping healthy**
  e.g. saving people from premature death by healthy living i.e. no drugs, exercise.

- **What humans and animals need to survive.**

- **Animal reproduction, endangered species, causes.**

- **How the changing environment affects animal life, global warming, melting ice caps, destruction of the rain forests.**

- **Food chains.**

- **What plants need to grow, how they get destroyed.**

- **Caring for the environment, pollution** e.g. land, air and sea.

- **Draw designs and diagrams.**

- **Ask questions** e.g. What happens if the rainforests continue to be cut down?

- **Discuss problems, find possible solutions to problems.**

#### SAVE THE PLANET

# Area of Concern

Name ............................................................ Class ........................................................

**AREA OF CONCERN** ....................................................................................

**What I know about the problem**

- ● ........................................................................................................................

- ● ........................................................................................................................

- ● ........................................................................................................................

- ● ........................................................................................................................

**How I can find out more** ............................................................................

- ● ........................................................................................................................

**What we can do about it** ............................................................................

1. ........................................................................................................................

2. ........................................................................................................................

3. ........................................................................................................................

4. ........................................................................................................................

5. ........................................................................................................................

**S A V E T H E P L A N E T**

## SAVE THE PLANET

## Newspaper Report

# GLOBAL DAILY NEWS

**Reporter** ................................................................

## SAVE THE PLANET

# Facts and Figures

**Name** ........................................................ **Class** ........................................................

**MY AREA OF CONCERN** ........................................................................................

| **FACTS** | **FIGURES** |
|---|---|
| | |

### SOURCES OF FACTS AND FIGURES

## SAVE THE PLANET
# Souvenirs

**Name** .......................................................... **Class** ..........................................................

**Badges**

**Post Card**

**Other Ideas**

.............................................................................................................................

.............................................................................................................................

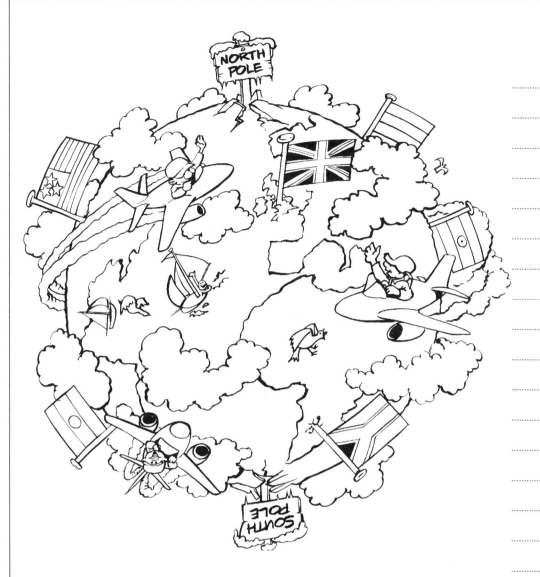

## PROJECT 4

# AROUND THE WORLD

**AROUND THE WORLD**

# Aims of the Project

● **For the children to learn about other countries.**

........................................................................................................

● **For the children to develop new skills.**

........................................................................................................

● **For the children to experience 'hands on' learning.**

........................................................................................................

● **For the children to develop confidence and self esteem.**

........................................................................................................

● **For the children to learn about enterprise.**

........................................................................................................

● **For the school to develop partners in the local community.**

........................................................................................................

● **For the staff to develop team work.**

........................................................................................................

● **For the staff to find creative ways of teaching.**

........................................................................................................

● **For the staff to find relevance in what they teach.**

........................................................................................................

● **For the staff to develop new skills.**

........................................................................................................

## AROUND THE WORLD

# What happens?

- Each class becomes a different country for a week.

- They read books, visit the library and go on the internet to find out about the countries they are studying.

- They go on visits to find out more about the country and what they will need to do to make the classroom look like that country.

- The children spend the week converting their classroom into that country with displays and friezes of countryside and places of interest, clothes, homes, language, crafts and souvenirs, food and drink, music and dance.

- They do 'hands on' practical activities e.g. craft, cooking, singing.

- They invite partners into school to help them.

- They visit the other classes in an 'Away Day'. They make passports and go through customs.

- At the end of the week they are involved in a musical performance with a foreign theme.

- Parents and partners can have the opportunity to buy souvenirs from around the world.

## AROUND THE WORLD
# Visits
### PLACES TO VISIT

● **Restaurants,** e.g. Indian, Chinese, Italian, French.

● **Supermarkets** e.g. Tesco, Sainsbury's, Asda.

● **China Towns in a major city.**

● **Mosques and other religious buildings.**

● **Craft centres.**

● **Museums.**

## VISITORS TO SCHOOL

● **People from other countries.**

● **Dance groups from other countries.**

● **Musicians from other countries.**

● **Chefs from foreign restaurants (school dinners could have a theme of 'Around the World').**

● **Craftsmen.**

## AROUND THE WORLD
# The Special Week

**FIRST DAY**
- Special assembly to introduce the week.

- Classes visit places of interest.

  The children make passports with their photos inside.

**ON GOING**
- Lessons are cross curricular and 'hands on'.

- Partners come into school and support the pupils.

- The children can contribute to a whole school mural for permanent display
  e.g. a collage map of the world.

**END OF THE WEEK**
- The children are involved in an 'Away day' at the school where they visit other classes and learn about other countries.

- The children can take part in musical workshops and perform for the rest of the school and the partners. A musician can be invited into school to work with the children and teach them songs from around the world. The children can learn to play foreign instruments e.g. African Drums.
  **or**
- The children may dress up in foreign costume and perform a cat walk show with music and dance. Parents and partners can be invited.

## AROUND THE WORLD

# 'Musical Extravaganza'

**At the end of the week the children and partners can be invited to a 'Musical Extravaganza'.**

● **The hall can be converted into an outdoor market square. The partners can sit at tables with fancy table cloths. There can be bunting and balloons, lanterns, palm trees/foreign scenes painted on the doors etc.**

● **The children and partners can be invited to a musical performance with a foreign theme. The children can dress up in national costume and perform a cat walk show.**

● **Partners will have the opportunity to buy souvenirs from the different countries**
e.g. post cards, pottery, lace crafts, painted glass, decorated pebbles, musical instruments, sweets.

## AROUND THE WORLD

# Literacy

## KEY STAGE 1

### ■ READING

● Read non-fiction books and learn about the difference between non-fiction and fiction.

● Read non-fiction geography books.

● Use dictionaries to find words associated with the topic.

● Make class dictionaries on the topic.

### ■ WRITING

● Write lists of words associated with the country you are studying.

● Draw and make labels and captions.

● Write a recount of the visit to the company.

● Write a glossary for the country you are studying.

● Produce simple flow charts.

● Write simple non chronological reports about the topic that is **being studied** e.g. clothes in India.

### ■ SPEAKING AND LISTENING

● **Questions** e.g. ask questions about the country.

● **Show and Tell** e.g. talk about the different food from that country.

● Discussion groups, opinions about the country.

● Tell stories about that country; read poems aloud.

# KEY STAGE 2

**READING**

● Understand the difference between fiction and non-fiction books.

● Locate information using contents and indexes.

● Identify and highlight or note key words from a text.

● Research the topic being undertaken.

**WRITING**

● Make notes from information books in different forms
e.g. flow charts, key words and lists.

● Write non-chronological reports.

● Write a recount of a visit to a company.

● Make alphabetically ordered texts for your country.

● Write tourist newspaper reports e.g. safari experience in Kenya.

● Write a point of view about your country
e.g. why women should not be allowed in the mosque with the men

● Design adverts for the country you are studying e.g. Come to France.

● Write a letter to someone as if you lived in that country e.g. you could imagine you were a French child.

● List cues for a talk you will be giving to the visitors at the end of the week about your country.

● Write a commentary for TV or radio on your time period.

● Write a balanced argument on the good/bad points of that country.

**SPEAKING AND LISTENING**

● Read and listen to poems and stories from that country.

● Hot Seat: e.g. Imagine you live in the country. The other children ask you questions about it.

● Discuss views and opinions about that country.

### AROUND THE WORLD

# Geography

## KNOWLEDGE, SKILLS & UNDERSTANDING

Enquiry and skills, knowledge and understanding of places, patterns and processes, environmental change and sustainable development

## BREADTH OF STUDY

## KEY STAGE 1/2

### PLACES AROUND THE WORLD

- **Maps – make a map of the world for the wall, colour in the country.**

- **Weather – What kind of weather do they have? Is it like ours?**

- **Homes - how other people live, what the houses are made of.**

- **Jobs - what they do, industry, shops, farming.**

- **Landscape, mountains, rivers, vegetation.**

- **Animals - endangered species.**

- **Currencies - use the coins, value compared to sterling.**

- **Food and drink - crops that are grown, food tasting, cooking.**

- **Language - learn to speak their language.**

- **Music & dance -  listen to, learn songs, use instruments, dance, anthems.**

- **Places of interest -  look at photos, books and videos, invite visitors.**

- **Religion & Festivals – religion, saints days.**

- **Transport – how the people travel around** e.g. sledges, rickshaws.

- **Clothes – how the climate affects the clothing, dress up.**

## AROUND THE WORLD
# Art & Design

## KNOWLEDGE, SKILLS AND UNDERSTANDING

Explore, develop ideas, investigate and make, evaluate and develop, knowledge and understanding

## BREADTH OF STUDY
## KEY STAGE 1/2 IDEAS

- Paint famous places.

- Collages of animals from that country

- Collages of people using fabrics and material.

- Paint glass and pebbles.

- Lace craft.

- Postcards from around the world, draw and colour.

- Prints using vegetables, card, polystyrene.

- Hieroglyphics/Chinese writing in ink.

- Greeting cards in another language.

- Flags of the country, attached to sticks or cane.

- Tie dye.

- Henna patterns.

- Menus for food in foreign restaurants.

- Tribal head dresses.

**AROUND THE WORLD**

# Design Technology

## KNOWLEDGE, SKILLS AND UNDERSTANDING

**Develop, plan and communicate ideas, work with tools and equipment, evaluate processes and products, knowledge and understanding of materials**

## BREADTH OF STUDY

## KEY STAGE 1/2 IDEAS

- **Design and make foreign instruments.**

- **Design and make masks.**

- **Design and make bracelets, necklaces.**

- **Design and make 3D homes** e.g. house on stilts, igloo, tent.

- **Design and make pottery.**

- **Design and make 3D models** e.g. Eiffel Tower, Taj Mahal.

- **Design and make a relief model of the country from papier mache.**

- **Design and make printing blocks.**

- **Design and make shadow puppets.**

- **Design and make rugs.**

- **Work with a variety of tools** e.g. brushes, scissors, glue.

- **Work with a variety of materials**
  e.g. lollipop sticks, cane, card, wood, plasticene, clay, foil, seeds, fabrics.

### AROUND THE WORLD
# Non-chronological Report

**Name** ........................................  **Class** ........................................

## PLACE ........................................

**Introduction** ........................................
........................................
........................................
........................................

**Heading 1** ........................................
........................................
........................................
........................................

**Heading 2** ........................................
........................................
........................................
........................................

**Heading 3** ........................................
........................................
........................................
........................................

**Conclusion** ........................................
........................................
........................................
........................................

### AROUND THE WORLD
# Postcards from the Country

**Name** ............................................ **Class** .......................................

## MY COUNTRY ...................................................................

Ideas – National costume, seaside, countryside, famous sights

### AROUND THE WORLD
# Instructions
### FOOD AND DRINK

**Name** .................................................................... **Class** ....................................................................

**My Country** ....................................................................

**How to make it** ....................................................................

## WHAT I WILL NEED

● ....................................................................

● ....................................................................

● ....................................................................

● ....................................................................

● ....................................................................

## HOW TO MAKE IT

1. ....................................................................

2. ....................................................................

3. ....................................................................

4. ....................................................................

5. ....................................................................

6. ....................................................................

### AROUND THE WORLD
# My Diary

**Name** .................................. **Holiday to** ..................................

## Day One

.....................................................................
.....................................................................
.....................................................................
.....................................................................
.....................................................................
.....................................................................
.....................................................................
.....................................................................
.....................................................................
.....................................................................
.....................................................................
.....................................................................

## Day Two

.....................................................................
.....................................................................
.....................................................................
.....................................................................
.....................................................................
.....................................................................
.....................................................................
.....................................................................
.....................................................................
.....................................................................
.....................................................................
.....................................................................

## Day Three

.....................................................................
.....................................................................
.....................................................................
.....................................................................
.....................................................................
.....................................................................
.....................................................................
.....................................................................
.....................................................................
.....................................................................

## Day Four

.....................................................................
.....................................................................
.....................................................................
.....................................................................
.....................................................................
.....................................................................
.....................................................................
.....................................................................
.....................................................................
.....................................................................

### AROUND THE WORLD
# Points of View

Name ........................................................ Class ..........................................................

## MY COUNTRY ..............................................................

| GOOD POINTS | BAD POINTS |
|---|---|
| ● .............................................. | ● .............................................. |
| ● .............................................. | ● .............................................. |
| ● .............................................. | ● .............................................. |
| ● .............................................. | ● .............................................. |
| ● .............................................. | ● .............................................. |

**Overall opinion – Would I live there?**

................................................................................................

................................................................................................

................................................................................................

................................................................................................

## PROJECT 5

# BACK IN TIME

**BACK IN TIME**

# Aims of the Project

- For the school to develop partners in the local community.

- For the staff to develop team work.

- For the staff to find creative ways of teaching.

- For the staff to find relevance in what they teach.

- For the staff to develop new skills.

- For the children to develop new skills.

- For the children to experience 'hands on' learning.

- For the children to develop confidence and self esteem.

- For the children learn about the history of the world.

**BACK IN TIME**

# What happens?

● **Each class focuses on a period in history** e.g. Vikings, Romans, Victorians.

● **They visit places of interest prior to the week to get ideas.**

● **They read books, visit the library and go on the internet to find out more.**

● **The children spend the week converting their classrooms into museum with displays, photos and friezes:**

     ▲ **Homes people lived in**

     ▲ **Clothes people wore**

     ▲ **Famous people**

     ▲ **Important events**

     ▲ **Schools**

     ▲ **Farming**

     ▲ **Wars**

● **They do 'hands on' practical activities.**

● **They invite partners into school to help them.**

● **They invite the rest of the school to visit their museum on the final day.**

**PROJECT 5:3**

### BACK IN TIME

# Places to Visit/Visitors

- **Museums**

......................................................................................................................

- **Historical cities/towns**

......................................................................................................................

- **Exhibitions**

......................................................................................................................

- **Transport museums**

......................................................................................................................

- **Motor museums**

......................................................................................................................

- **Museums of childhood**

......................................................................................................................

- **Archaeological sites**

......................................................................................................................

**BACK IN TIME**

# The Special Week

**FIRST DAY**
● Special assembly to introduce the week.

● Classes visit places of interest.

**ON GOING**
● Lessons are cross curricular and 'hands on'.

● Pupils make things for the museum.

● Pupils make items to sell at the museum.

● Partners come into school and support the pupils.

**FINAL DAY**
● Each class visits the museums.

● Staff and children are given a guided tour.

● They can buy souvenirs at the museum.

● Each class contributes to photographs and reports for a special book, called 'Our Museum', which will be displayed in the school.

**BACK IN TIME**

# Museum Day

● **Each class invites the others to visit their museum.**

.................................................................................................................

● **The children tour each museum looking at what there is and talk to representatives from the class:**

⟁ **look at the displays** ............................................................

⟁ **look at the posters** .............................................................

⟁ **look at the photographs** .......................................................

⟁ **look at facts and figures** ......................................................

⟁ **look at reports** ..................................................................

⟁ **look at video evidence** ........................................................

● **Visitors to the museum can buy souvenirs the children have made**
e.g. Egyptian jewellery, Victorian wooden toys, Aztec designs, Roman tiles, Egyptian mummy cases, Viking long boats.

.................................................................................................................

● **Each class contributes to a book called 'Our Museum' which will then be put on display in the school.**

.................................................................................................................

.................................................................................................................

## BACK IN TIME

# Literacy

## LITERACY KEY STAGE 1

### READING

● Read non-fiction books and learn about the difference between non-fiction and fiction.

● Read non-fiction history books.

● Use dictionaries to find words associated with the topic.

● Make class dictionaries on the topic.

### WRITING

● Write lists of words associated with your time period.

● Draw and make labels and captions for your exhibits.

● Write a recount of the visit to a museum.

● Write a glossary for the time period you are studying.

● **Produce simple flow charts** e.g. changes in transport.

● **Write simple non-chronological reports about the topic that is being studied** e.g. Victorian toys.

### SPEAKING AND LISTENING

● **Show and tell:** e.g. bring in old toys.

● Read aloud non-fiction books.

● Discuss old photographs and old objects.

● Act out an old school day.

# KEY STAGE 2

## READING

● **Understand the difference between fiction and non-fiction books.**

● **Locate information using contents and indexes.**

● **Identify and highlight or note key words from a text.**

● **Research the topic being undertaken.**

## WRITING

● **Make notes from information books in different forms,** e.g. flow charts, key words and lists

● **Write non-chronological reports** e.g. weapons.

● **Write a recount of a visit to a museum or historical building.**

● **Make alphabetically ordered texts for your time period.**

● **Write historical newspaper reports** e.g. Queen Victoria dies.

● **Write a point of view about your time period** e.g. Why should all men go to war?

● **Design adverts depicting the era you are studying** e.g. Egyptian jewellery.

● **Write a letter to someone as if you lived in those days** e.g. you could imagine you were a chimney sweep or you are in the trenches during the First World War.

● **List cues for a talk you will be giving to the visitors at the end of the week about your time in history.**

● **Write a commentary for TV or radio on your time period.**

● **Write a balanced argument on the good/bad points of living in that time period.**

## SPEAKING AND LISTENING

● **Ask questions; share answers.**

● **Show and Tell:** e.g. bring in items from the Second World War.

● **Hot Seat:** e.g. imagine you are Henry VIII being questioned on your life.

● **Read aloud and listen to information from non-fiction books.**

## BACK IN TIME

# History

## KNOWLEDGE, SKILLS & UNDERSTANDING

Chronological understanding, knowledge and understanding of events, people and changes in the past, historical interpretation and enquiry, organisation and communication.

## BREADTH OF STUDY

## KEY STAGE 1/2

● **Invite grandparents, local people into school to talk about their lives.**

● **Use sources of information** e.g. photographs, videos, internet, library.

● **Sequence order of events.**

● **Visit historical buildings and museums.**

● **Invite players and performers into school to re-enact historical events.**

● **Read, write, discuss, make and design.**

● **Learn about famous people in history** e.g. Christopher Columbus, Vincent Van Gogh, St Francis, Guy Fawkes and the Gunpowder Plot.

● **Learn about different periods in history** i.e. the Romans, Anglo-Saxons, Vikings, Victorian Britain, Britain since the 1930s, Ancient Greece, Ancient Egypt, Aztecs.

● **Look at how the people lived** e.g. famous people, homes, transport, entertainment, war, school, toys and games, towns, inventions.

● **Newspaper reports from a period in history.**

● **Family trees.**

## BACK IN TIME

# Art & Design

## KNOWLEDGE, SKILLS AND UNDERSTANDING

Explore, develop ideas, investigate and make, evaluate and develop, knowledge and understanding

## BREADTH OF STUDY

## KEY STAGE 1 IDEAS

- **Collage of famous painters' work** e.g. Van Gogh, Picasso.

- **Draw and paint old toys.**

- **Draw your own family tree.**

- **Life size paintings of people in old costumes using different fabrics.**

- **Picture poscards from Victorian times.**

- **Stone rubbings of old houses.**

- **Tapestry, needlecraft.**

## KEY STAGE 2 IDEAS

- **Copy/trace old black and white photographs, draw with charcoal.**

- **Old manuscripts by dipping paper in tea bag juice.**

- **Charcoal pictures of famous people.**

- **Wax resist paintings of the Blitz.**

- **Collage of Roman soldiers using coloured foil.**

- **Chalk pictures of Roman shields.**

- **Life size paintings of Greek Gods.**

- **Egyptian masks with seeds and shiny paper.**

- **Egyptian/Viking jewellery using card and seeds.**

- **Hieroglyphic writing with pens.**

- **Tudor portraits.**

BACK IN TIME

# Design Technology

## KNOWLEDGE, SKILLS AND UNDERSTANDING

Develop, plan and communicate ideas, work with tools and equipment, evaluate processes and products, knowledge and understanding of materials

## BREADTH OF STUDY

## KEY STAGE 1/2 IDEAS

- Design and make old toys.

- Make 3D models of old vehicles.

- Design and make an Egyptian coffin with a lid which opens.

- Design and make a 3D Egyptian pyramid.

- Design and make Viking long boats, helmets, shields.

- Design and make battle axes from rolled up newspaper and card.

- Design and make a 3D model of a Roman town, Greek/Egyptian village.

- Design and make Greek masks.

- Design and make Greek pillars and temples.

- Design and make Roman tiles.

- Design and make Tudor houses out of boxes.

- **Work with a variety of tools** e.g. brushes, scissors, glue.

- **Work with a variety of materials** e.g. food cartons, shoe boxes, plastic bottles, egg cartons, yogurt cartons, silver foil, toilet rolls, bubble wrap, plastic cups, cotton reels, off cuts of wood.

- Use tools to cut, fold, glue, saw, sew and join.

## BACK IN TIME

# Hisorical News Report

# HISTORICAL DAILY TELEGRAPH

**Reporter** .................................................................

**BACK IN TIME**

# Non-chronological Report

Name ............................................................ Class ............................................................

## PERIOD IN HISTORY ............................................................

Introduction ............................................................

............................................................

............................................................

............................................................

Heading 1 ............................................................

............................................................

............................................................

............................................................

Heading 2 ............................................................

............................................................

............................................................

............................................................

Heading 3 ............................................................

............................................................

............................................................

............................................................

Conclusion ............................................................

............................................................

............................................................

............................................................

### BACK IN TIME
# Points of View

Name _____     Class _____

## PERIOD IN HISTORY _____

| GOOD POINTS | BAD POINTS |
|---|---|
| ● | ● |
| ● | ● |
| ● | ● |
| ● | ● |
| ● | ● |

**Overall opinion - Would I have liked to have lived in those days?**

## BACK IN TIME
# A Letter from Long Ago

## PROJECT 6

# TOWN OF THE FUTURE

### 6:2 AIMS OF THE PROJECT
### 6:3 WHAT HAPPENS
### 6:4 PLACES TO VISIT
### 6:5 THE SPECIAL WEEK
### 6:6 EXHIBITION DAY
### 6:7 CURRICULUM IDEAS

## TOWN OF THE FUTURE

# Aims of the Project

● **For the children to develop new skills.**

● **For the children to experience 'hands on' learning.**

● **For the children to develop confidence and self esteem.**

● **For the children to develop a positive outlook for the future.**

● **For the school to develop partners in the local community.**

● **For the staff to develop team work.**

● **For the staff to find creative ways of teaching.**

● **For the staff to find relevance in what they teach.**

● **For the staff to develop new skills.**

**PROJECT 6:2**

**TOWN OF THE FUTURE**

# What happens?

- **Each class focuses on an area of a town** e.g. school, housing estate, shops, factories, leisure.

- **They read books, visit the library and go on the internet to find out more.**

- **They visit a company prior to the week to get ideas.**

- **They visit places in their town to find out more about their area.**

- **They design and make their part of the town set in the future.**

- **They invite partners into school to help them.**

- **They set up an exhibition in the hall of their town of the future.**

- **They invite the rest of the school and partners to visit the display and talk about the future of the town.**

## TOWN OF THE FUTURE
# Visits

**Each class can visit different places to help them make their designs.**
**Examples:**

● **Shopping centres**

● **Supermarkets**

● **Airports**

● **Railway Stations**

● **Ambulance Stations**

● **Fire Stations**

● **Police Stations**

● **Hospitals**

● **Leisure Centres**

● **New Housing Developments**

● **Factories**

## TOWN OF THE FUTURE
# The Special Week

**FIRST DAY**
- Special assembly to introduce the week.

........................................................................

- Classes visit companies.

........................................................................

**ON GOING**
- Classes design and make their models.

........................................................................

- Lessons are cross curricular.

........................................................................

- Partners come into school and support the companies.

........................................................................

**FINAL DAY**
- The models are displayed in the hall.

........................................................................

- Parents and partners are invited to see the displays.

........................................................................

## TOWN OF THE FUTURE
# Display Day

● The products need to be finished by the penultimate day.

● On the last morning class representatives set up tables in the hall to display their part of the town.

● The models can be displayed together as a whole town or they can be displayed separately. The models will be labelled.

● Parents and partners are invited to the event.

● Representatives from the local borough council, local councillors and politicians can be invited to the event.

● Class representatives can talk about their part of the town while everyone else listens.

● There can be a 'Question Time' where the children can ask the local borough council/ politicians about the future of the town and if any of their ideas will ever be used. The visitors can ask questions of class representatives. (Representatives could be seated on the school stage)

● After the event a display area can be set up in the entrance hall or in classrooms as a reminder of the special project.

# TOWN OF THE FUTURE
# Literacy
## KEY STAGE 1

### READING
- Read non-fiction books and learn about the difference between non-fiction and fiction.
- Read non-fiction books about homes, houses and buildings.
- Use dictionaries to find words associated with the topic.
- Make class dictionaries on the topic.

### WRITING
- Write lists of things you need for making the models.
- Write lists of words associated with the town of the future.
- Write instructions for making a model.
- Draw and make labels and captions for the models.
- Write a recount of the visit to the company.
- Write a glossary for the area of the town you are learning about.
- Produce simple flow charts.
- Write simple non chronological reports about the topic that is being studied
  e.g. houses, bungalows, semi detached, flats.

### SPEAKING AND LISTENING
- Ask questions about what is to be made, and how it will be made.
- Show and tell what has been made.
- **Hot Seat:** e.g. answer questions about your design.

## KEY STAGE 2

### READING

- Understand the difference between fiction and non-fiction books.

- Locate information using contents and indexes.

- Identify and highlight key words from a text.

- Research the topic being undertaken.

### WRITING

- **Make notes from information books in different forms** e.g. flow charts, key words and list.

- **Write non-chronological reports** e.g. different forms of leisure – cinema, ice skating, bowling.

- **Write instructions for making models** e.g. how you made the school.

- **Write a recount of a visit to a company.**

- **Make alphabetically ordered texts** e.g. for a house, an attic, a bedroom...

- **Write newspaper reports about the town of the future,**
  e.g. giving information on what it has, what it can do, what people think of it.

- **Write explanations of how a particular aspect of the town works.**

- **Write a point of view of why something is excellent** e.g. your home of the future.

- **Design adverts selling** e.g. the house of the future.

- **Write a letter to a friend on a different planet telling them about your part of the town.**

- **Write a balanced argument on the good/bad points.**

### SPEAKING AND LISTENING

- Group discussion about what is to be made: brainstorming.

- Views and opinions for designs: reasons.

- Give a talk to the visitors about your part of the town.

- Give a commentary for TV or radio on the wonderful aspects of your town.

## TOWN OF THE FUTURE

# Art & Design

## KNOWLEDGE, SKILLS AND UNDERSTANDING

Explore, develop ideas, investigate and make, evaluate and develop, knowledge and understanding

## BREADTH OF STUDY

## KEY STAGE 1/2 IDEAS

- Look at non-fiction books of famous buildings and the architects.

- Look at science fiction videos, magazines and books for ideas.

- Pictures/paintings of the town of the future.

- Silhouettes of the buildings.

- Collages of the buildings.

- Labelled diagrams of buildings, rooms.

- Draw bird's eye view of buildings.

- **Adverts** e.g. building for sale.

- Plan of the inside of the building, drawn to scale and labelled.

- Use ICT to draw pictures of the buildings.

- Colour comparisons, looking at colours that contrast etc.

- Experiment with a range of materials suitable for the building.

## TOWN OF THE FUTURE

# Design Technology

## KNOWLEDGE, SKILLS AND UNDERSTANDING

Develop, plan and communicate ideas, work with tools and equipment, evaluate processes and products, knowledge and understanding of materials

## BREADTH OF STUDY

## KEY STAGE 1/2 IDEAS

- Design and make a building of the future.

- Design and make a park of the future.

- Design and make a fun fair of the future.

- Design and make a form of transport of the future.

- Design and make a school of the future.

- Design and make an entertainment complex of the future.

- Design and make a station, airport of the future.

- Design and make a fire station of the future.

- Design and make a hospital of the future.

- **Work with a variety of tools** e.g. brushes, scissors, glue.

- **Work with a variety of materials** e.g. food cartons, shoe boxes, plastic bottles, egg cartons, yogurt cartons, silver foil, toilet rolls, bubble wrap, plastic cups, cotton reels, off cuts of wood.

- **Use tools to cut, fold, glue, saw and join.**

## TOWN OF THE FUTURE

# Numeracy

## KNOWLEDGE, SKILLS AND UNDERSTANDING

Number, shape space and measure, handling data

## BREADTH OF STUDY

## KEY STAGE 1 IDEAS

- Count how many windows, doors etc.

- Use a ruler to draw and measure lines to the nearest cm for the building you are designing

- **Compare two lengths** e.g. How long is this building, how long is the other?

- **Use language to describe 2D and 3D shapes ie the shapes of the buildings you have designed** e.g. It is a triangular pyramid.

- **Estimate, measure and compare shapes you have drawn** e.g. compare the size of one building to another.

- **Use language to describe position, direction and movement** e.g. Where is the building? What direction is it facing?

## KEY STAGE 2 IDEAS

- Use fractions and decimals to get accurate measurements of the buildings you are drawing.

- How many faces? How many edges?

- Identify lines of symmetry in your buildings.

- Identify right angles and parallel lines in the buildings you draw.

- Visualize how the building will look in 3D from a 2D drawing.

- Use a protractor to draw and measure angles of your designs.

- What is the area and perimeter of the building?

## TOWN OF THE FUTURE
# Advertisement

Name _____

# HOUSE OF THE FUTURE

| KITCHEN | BEDROOM |
|---|---|
|  |  |

| BATHROOM |  |
|---|---|
|  |  |

### TOWN OF THE FUTURE
# Explanation

**Name** .......................................................... **Class** ..........................................................

**Explain how something works in the future** e.g. a form of transport, a household appliance

**What is it?** ..........................................................

**How it works** ..........................................................

..........................................................

..........................................................

..........................................................

..........................................................

..........................................................

..........................................................

..........................................................

..........................................................

..........................................................

## DIAGRAM

#### TOWN OF THE FUTURE

# Non-chronological Report

**Name** .................................................. **Class** ..................................................

**Introduction** ..................................................
..................................................
..................................................
..................................................

**Buildings** ..................................................
..................................................
..................................................
..................................................

**Jobs** ..................................................
..................................................
..................................................
..................................................

**Schools** ..................................................
..................................................
..................................................
..................................................

**Transport** ..................................................
..................................................
..................................................
..................................................

## PROJECT 7

# TECHNO RALLY

**TECHNO RALLY**

# Aims of the Project

- For the children to experience a techno rally.

- For the children to develop new skills.

- For the children to experience 'hands on' learning.

- For the children to develop confidence and self esteem.

- For the school to develop partners in the local community.

- For the staff to develop team work.

- For the staff to find creative ways of teaching.

- For the staff to find relevance in what they teach.

- For the staff to develop new skills.

## TECHNO RALLY

# What happens?

- Classes build vehicles and compete to see which go the furthest.

- They visit a company prior to the week for ideas.

- They test different materials to find the most suitable.

- They design and make their vehicles.

- They invite partners into school to help them.

- They have a Techno Rally at the end of the week to find the models which travel the furthest.

## TECHNO RALLY

# Making the Vehicles

- **All vehicles must not have an engine.**

- **They can be different types of vehicles**
  e.g. sports cars, fire engines, trucks, tractors, tanks, trams, tanker, sand yacht.

- **They can be made out of different materials**
  e.g. card, cardboard, boxes or plastic washing up bottles.

- **Wheels can be made out of different materials**
  e.g. wood, plastic, card, cotton reels.

- **Wheel attachments can be made of different materials**
  e.g. dowel, paint brushes, straws, felt tipped pen barrels.

**PROJECT 7:4**

**TECHNO RALLY**

# Places to Visit

**Each class visits a company to look at vehicles and how they are made
Examples:**

● **Motor Museums**

.................................................................................................................

● **Bus stations**

.................................................................................................................

● **Coach firms**

.................................................................................................................

● **Royal Mail**

.................................................................................................................

● **Fire Stations**

.................................................................................................................

● **Police Stations**

.................................................................................................................

● **Ambulance service**

.................................................................................................................

● **Car dealers**

.................................................................................................................

● **Trams**

.................................................................................................................

● **Truck companies**

.................................................................................................................

## TECHNO RALLY

# The Rally

- **The vehicles need to be finished by the penultimate day.**

- **A ramp is set up on the yard for the vehicles**
  (The ramp can be made of a large sheet of plywood resting on a step ladder or box).

- **Distance markers are set up.**

- **On the last day everyone goes onto the school yard for the rally.**

- **Each class lines up with their vehicles.**

- **The children take it in turn to roll their vehicle down the ramp. Distances are recorded.**
  N.B. They are not allowed to push their vehicles.

- **Vehicles in each class that travel the furthest receive prizes.**

- **The vehicles can be put on display in the school.**

- **Children can record the distances travelled and take photographs for a display book.**

PROJECT 7:6

**TECHNO RALLY**

# The Special Week

**FIRST DAY**
● Special assembly to introduce the Techno Rally.

● Classes visit companies (or in previous week).

**ON GOING**
● A ramp is designed for the vehicles to go down.

● Classes design and make their vehicles.

● Lessons are cross curricular.

● Partners come into school to help.

**FINAL DAY**
● Children, Parents and partners attend the Techno Rally Event.
The distance vehicles travel is measured and there are winners from each class.

## TECHNO RALLY

# Literacy

### KEY STAGE 1

## ■ READING

- Read non-fiction books and learn about the difference between non-fiction and fiction.

- Read non-fiction books about transport and vehicles.

- Use dictionaries to find words associated with the topic.

- Make class dictionaries on the topic.

## ■ WRITING

- Write lists of things you need for making the vehicles.

- Write lists of words associated with your vehicle.

- Write instructions for making your vehicle.

- Draw and make labels and captions for the vehicles.

- Write a recount of the visit to the company.

- Write a glossary for the vehicles you are making.

- Produce simple flow charts.

- Write simple non-chronological reports about the topic that is being studied e.g. trucks.

## ■ SPEAKING AND LISTENING

- Show and Tell: How your vehicle was made; how it works.

- Ask questions about the materials to be used.

- Give reasons for the choice of materials.

## KEY STAGE 2

### READING

- Understand the difference between fiction and non-fiction books.

- Read non-fiction books about transport and vehicles.

- Read instruction books about how to make models and vehicles.

- Locate information using contents and indexes.

- Identify and highlight or note key words from a text.

- Research the topic being undertaken.

### WRITING

- **Make notes from information books in different forms** e.g. flow charts, key words and lists.

- **Write non-chronological reports** e.g. different types of trucks.

- Use technical language when writing reports.

- Write instructions for making your vehicles.

- Write a recount of a visit to a company.

- Make alphabetically ordered texts for your vehicles.

- Write newspaper reports about your vehicle
  e.g. giving information about it and what people think of it.

- Write explanations of how your vehicle works.

- Write about why the vehicles your class made are the best.

- Design adverts selling your vehicles.

- Write a commentary for TV or radio on your vehicles.

- Write a balanced argument on the good/bad points of the product.

### SPEAKING AND LISTENING

- Ask questions about the design: problems: how to solve them.

- Prepare an explanation of how your vehicle was made.

- Give views/opinions/reasons for following a certain design.

## TECHNO RALLY

# Numeracy

## KNOWLEDGE, SKILLS AND UNDERSTANDING

Number, shape space and measure, handling data

### BREADTH OF STUDY

### KEY STAGE 1 IDEAS

● **Use a ruler to draw and measure lines to the nearest cm.**

● **Compare two lengths** e.g. How long?

● **Use language to describe 2D and 3D shapes ie the shapes of the vehicles you have designed** e.g. cylinders, cuboids.

● **Estimate, measure and compare shapes you have drawn**
e.g. compare the size of another model someone else is making.

● **Measure the distance your vehicle travels, compare it to another.**

## KEY STAGE 2 IDEAS

● **Use fractions and decimals to get accurate measurements of the vehicle you are drawing.**

● **Use standard units of measure to draw your vehicle.**

● **Identify lines of symmetry in your vehicle.**

● **Identify right angles and parallel lines in your vehicle.**

● **Visualize how the vehicle will look in 3D from a 2D drawing.**

● **Use a protractor to draw and measure angles of your designs.**

● **Identify shapes on designs.**

## TECHNO RALLY

# Design Technology

### KNOWLEDGE, SKILLS AND UNDERSTANDING

Develop, plan and communicate ideas, work with tools and equipment, evaluate processes and products, knowledge and understanding of materials

### BREADTH OF STUDY

### KEY STAGE 1/2 IDEAS

- **Design and make a truck.**

- **Design and make a three wheeled vehicle.**

- **Design and make an open topped car.**

- **Design and make a sand yacht.**

- **Design and make a go cart.**

- **Design and make a tanker.**

- **Design and make an emergency vehicle** e.g. fire engine.

- **Work with a variety of tools** e.g. brushes, scissors, glue, compass.

- **Work with a variety of materials** e.g. food cartons, shoe boxes, plastic cartons, toilet rolls, plastic cups, cotton reels.

TECHNO RALLY

# Science

## KNOWLEDGE, SKILLS AND UNDERSTANDING

Scientific enquiry, life processes and living things, materials, physical processes

## BREADTH OF STUDY

## KEY STAGE 1/2 IDEAS

- **Forces** – make vehicles which need to be pushed to move.

- **Materials** – investigate types of materials suitable for making vehicles, how the sizes and shapes affect the speed and movement, investigate types of wheels to be used on the vehicle.

- Draw designs and diagrams.

- Investigate what may happen when you have made the vehicle.

- Test ideas using evidence from observations and measurement.

- **Ask questions** e.g. What will happen if I...?

- Investigate different surfaces on which the vehicles move the furthest.

- Investigate wheels made from different materials.

- Investigate whether vehicles move further if they are lighter or heavier.

### TECHNO RALLY

# Non-chronological Report

**Name** ................................................... **Class** ...................................................

## TITLE: VEHICLE ...................................................

e.g. cars, lorries, tractors, tankers, buses, trams, fire engines, ambulances

**Introduction** ...................................................

...................................................

...................................................

...................................................

**Heading 1** ...................................................

...................................................

...................................................

...................................................

**Heading 2** ...................................................

...................................................

...................................................

...................................................

**Heading 3** ...................................................

...................................................

...................................................

...................................................

**Heading 4** ...................................................

...................................................

...................................................

...................................................

## TECHNO RALLY

# Vehicle Design

**Name** ............................................................  **Class** ............................................................

**Ideas - sports car, three wheeler, sand yacht, truck, tanker, tank**

## TECHNO RALLY

# Instructions

## HOW TO MAKE THE VEHICLE

**Name** .................................................  **Class** .................................................

**My Vehicle** .................................................

**How to make it** .................................................

## WHAT I WILL NEED

● .................................................

● .................................................

● .................................................

● .................................................

● .................................................

### My Vehicle

## HOW TO MAKE IT

1. .................................................

2. .................................................

3. .................................................

4. .................................................

5. .................................................

6. .................................................

     Published by Horizons (UK) Ltd

# SUPER LEARNING PROJECT - WHOLE SCHOOL PREPARATION

**THEME**

**DATE**

**STAFF MEETINGS**

**ACTIVITIES**

**RESOURCES**

**MARKETING**

**BUSINESS LINKS**

**PARENT/GOVERNOR INVOLVEMENT**

# SUPER LEARNING PROJECT - PLANNING SHEET: ONE

| THEME | | | CLASS |
|---|---|---|---|
| **TEACHER** | | | |

| | | | |
|---|---|---|---|
| **MONDAY** | | | |
| **TUESDAY** | | | |
| **WEDNESDAY** | | | |
| **THURSDAY** | | | |
| **FRIDAY** | | | |

# SUPER LEARNING PROJECT - TEACHER PLANNING SHEET: TWO

**THEME**

**TEACHER**

**CLASS**

**LITERACY**

**NUMERACY**

**SUPER LEARNING PROJECT**

**ICT**

**SCIENCE**

# SUPER LEARNING PROJECT - TEACHER PLANNING SHEET (VAK activities)

| THEME | | TEACHER | | CLASS |
|---|---|---|---|---|

| | VISUAL ACTIVITIES | AUDITORY ACTIVITIES | KINAESTHETIC ACTIVITIES |
|---|---|---|---|
| LITERACY | | | |
| NUMERACY | | | |
| SCIENCE | | | |
| OTHERS | | | |

# Support

| THEME | DATE |
|---|---|
| TEACHER | CLASS |

## BUSINESS SUPPORT
e.g. visits to companies, visitors to school, business financial support

## CLASSROOM SUPPORT
e.g. parents, governors, public services

## ACTIVITIES TO SHARE WITH PARENTS, GOVERNORS, LOCAL COMMUNITY
e.g. dance, drama, craft, special event, open day

# Pupil Evaluation

Name _____ Class _____

Company _____

What we made _____

_____

_____

I liked it when... _____

_____

_____

It was fun when... _____

_____

_____

I learned how to... _____

_____

_____

The best part was... _____

_____

_____